FEATS of 21st-CENTURY ENGINEERING

21st-CENTURY TRAINS

Enslow Publishing
101 W. 23rd Street
Suite 240
New York, NY 10011
USA
enslow.com

Vera J. Hurst

Published in 2019 by Enslow Publishing, LLC.
101 W. 23rd Street, Suite 240, New York, NY 10011

Library of Congress Cataloging-in-Publication Data

Names: Hurst, Vera J., author.
Title: 21st century trains / Vera J. Hurst.
Description: New York, NY : Enslow Publishing, LLC., 2019. | Series: Feats of 21st century engineering | Includes bibliographical references and index. | Audience: 3-6.
Identifiers: LCCN 2017051684| ISBN 9780766097094 (library bound) | ISBN 9780766097100 (pbk.)
Subjects: LCSH: Railroad trains–Juvenile literature. | Locomotives–Technological innovations–Juvenile literature.
Classification: LCC TF148 .H87 2019 | DDC 625.2–dc23
LC record available at https://lccn.loc.gov/2017051684

Printed in the United States of America

To Our Readers: We have done our best to make sure all website addresses in this book were active and appropriate when we went to press. However, the author and the publisher have no control over and assume no liability for the material available on those websites or on any websites they may link to. Any comments or suggestions can be sent by e-mail to cu stomerservice@enslow.com.

Photo Credits: Cover, p. 1 (technical drawing) pluie_r/Shutterstock.com; cover, p. 1 (high speed train) Scanrail1/Shutterstock.com; p. 4 Xinhua News Agency/Getty Images; p. 9 Science & Society Picture Library/Getty Images; pp. 10-11 Omikron/Science Source/Getty Images; p. 13 ullstein bild/Getty Images; p. 17 Print Collector/Hulton Archive/Getty Images; p. 19 Pattarawit Chompipat/Alamy Stock Vector; p. 22 Library of Congress/Corbis Historical/Getty Images; pp. 24–25 Pool/Getty Images; pp. 26–27 Kurita Kaku/Gamma-Rapho/Getty Images; p. 30 Chandan Khanna/AFP/Getty Images; pp. 32–33 MartinMojzis/Shutterstock.com; p. 35 Antonius Egurnov/Shutterstock.com; p. 37 Peter Steffen/dpa/picturealliance/Newscom; p. 38 dpa picture alliance/Alamy Stock Photo; p. 41 AFP/A.Leung/Newscom.

CONTENTS

Twenty-first-century trains, like China's newest high-speed train, pictured above, promise exciting new ways to travel.

Introduction

From the beginning of history, humans have traveled. They have walked and carried all they owned on their backs. They followed food and found shelter wherever they could. They learned that carrying their property was hard. They decided to find a better way.

As people settled in villages, they had to trade to get what they needed. They had to find ways to move food and materials. People wanted to move from one place to another. Creative people had to develop new ways of traveling.

In some parts of the world, people transported things by camel trains. In other parts of the world, people used dogsleds. As more and more people moved around the world, they found ways to make bigger boats that could carry people and goods over water. They developed steam engines to transport things faster over land and sea. They invented airplanes to move people and cargo through the skies. They found other kinds of power and better designs to improve transportation. They faced challenges and found solutions to improve transportation, and they haven't stopped.

The invention of the train caused a big change in American society. Train travel made life much easier. It connected one coast to the other. These changes affected how we live today. Think about how life was when the only way to move coal to a ship was by wagons pulled by horses on rails. Now, some trains travel more than 124 miles per hour (200 kilometers/hour). Each time a successful solution to a problem was found, it led to even better travel options for the future.

Solving problems created a new area of study called engineering. Around the world today, engineers come up with answers to problems. They create new and better equipment. New rail engineering feats will transport people and goods faster. There will be fewer accidents. Passengers will travel more comfortably. Future trains will use less energy. They will be more environmentally friendly.

Engineers ask questions. They use basic principles of engineering to discover answers for problems. They follow specific steps to test solutions. Engineers design new ways of doing everyday tasks. They examine many ways to make their designs work. They experiment with many designs that may use different materials. Engineers test their ideas. After many trials and failures, they decide on a course of action. All the data they have gathered is used before they decide on a new design. This is what an engineer does every day.

Trains are a great way for people to travel across the county. They move tons of freight every day. High-speed rail systems transport cargo and people at 124 to 270 mph (200 to 435 kph). Freight arrives swiftly and safely on high-speed rail systems. Powerful magnets, like what hold your school papers on the refrigerator, pull trains in Japan and China with less environmental impact. Engineering improvements are what will make the trains of tomorrow much better.

Some students will decide to study hard and become engineers. Wouldn't it be exciting to be on the team that designed a vacuum tube train-travel system? This idea was developed by George Medhurst in 1799 but has not yet been created. It needs creative thinkers to find a way to engineer it. Could you be one of those thinkers?

1

From Horse-Drawn Carts to Electric Trains

Where did the idea come from that a cart could be placed in a groove or on a rail, making it easier to pull? Imagine someone who got tired because he had to haul large loads over long distances. Perhaps he sat down and envisioned how much easier it could be. When a cart is dragged along the ground, it creates a lot of friction. Friction is the resistance that happens when one object rubs against another. This early engineer might have added wheels to the cart. This lessened the resistance. Thus, the cart was easier to pull.

Early Beginnings

The ancient Greeks were the first to carve grooves into granite rocks specifically to transport goods over land. They designed wheels to fit inside the grooves and added them to wooden carts. Horses pulled the carts. These carts carried large ships over the Isthmus of Corinth to the sea. The earliest recorded date for this kind of rutway was 600 BCE.

Inventors found that using horses, oxen, or mules to pull carts in ruts had many problems. Wooden wheels would wear out. Animals had to be fed. Hills and mountains proved to be difficult to pass. The trips were slow, dangerous, and expensive.

The Age of Steam

Thomas Newcomen developed the first steam-powered engine used by a business in 1705. A steam engine is a machine that heats water in a boiler. Once the water is heated the steam can be used to move parts of a machine.

In the 1700s and 1800s, manufacturing grew rapidly. Engineers studied better ways to move coal, wood, and materials. They wanted goods to travel between places using less money and fuel. Manufacturing needs drove inventors to race toward better designs.

The first steam engines were used to pump water from mines. They were large and stationary. They used wood, then coal, as fuel. Changes to the early designs had to be made so that steam engines could be moved. Engines had to be made smaller and lighter. They had to fit on a cart-like platform. They had to become powerful enough to pull heavy loads.

In 1784, James Watt invented a steam engine that used less fuel and was lighter. This inspired Richard Trevithick of Wales to design the first steam locomotive in 1804. His locomotive pulled seventy men and 10 tons (9 metric tons) of iron nearly 10 miles (16 km) at 5 mph (8 kph). Imagine eight minivans stacked on a wheeled cart pulled by an invention no one had ever seen before. This amazing accomplishment marked the real beginning of mechanized train travel.

Even though Trevithick carried passengers on his first trip, the main purpose of trains during this time was to carry freight. Engineers worked to improve everything from brakes to train rails. They studied how to hook many cars together safely using a joint called a coupling. Solutions to these problems resulted in flanged wheels, new track rail designs, and innovative ways of building up soil.

Richard Trevithick built the first steam engine. Its successful operation led other engineers to improve upon his design.

Engineers figured out how to build strong, wooden boxes on the wheeled cart frames. These were later called freight cars, or bogies. Later, these freight cars were made from iron and steel to carry even heavier loads.

Let's Move!

In the 1800s, trains were the best way to transport people and things long distances all over the world. Trains carried people to new homes. They transported guns, ammunition, and troops in wars. They brought food and supplies over mountains and rivers.

On May 10, 1869, Leland Stanford drove the last spike into a rail on Promontory Summit in the Utah territory. The spike joined the rails of the first transcontinental railroad. It meant that a railroad connected most of the United States, from Pennsylvania to California. The transcontinental railroad allowed goods and passengers to travel across the United States more easily. In the past, goods going from one coast to the other had to travel on ships all the way around Cape Horn, at the southern tip of South America. The 15,000-mile (24,140-km) trip took from three to six months. It was a very dangerous journey. Train travel was safer and faster.

Few people understood how much their lives would change as they watched the last, golden spike being driven into the rails of the first Transcontinental Railway.

Nuclear Trains

When nuclear power was discovered, some engineers thought that it could be an exciting new way to power locomotives. In the 1950s, Dr. Lyle B. Borst and his students came up with a solution to train travel's fuel issues: nuclear-powered trains. Then they discovered that the radiation from nuclear power could hurt people. This meant that the locomotive needed to be made with heavy walls. These walls would protect people from the radiation. They designed a locomotive and named it the X-12. The locomotive would have weighed 360 tons (326 metric tons) and been 360 feet (110 meters) long! Due to cost and safety problems, the idea was soon scrapped.

When people first started riding on trains, they sat in open-air cars on wooden benches or they stood. Imagine how uncomfortable that would be on long journeys. Sometimes, sparks from wood-fired and coal-fired boilers landed on passengers' clothing and set them on fire. Soot and smoke caused coughing and eye pain. These issues had to be addressed before train travel would become safe and comfortable.

George Pullman formed a company in 1862 to take care of this problem. He designed passenger cars that were more useful. Seats could be made into beds or folded down from above like a bunk bed.

1900s to 2000: Wars and Industry

Steam locomotives were very popular until World War II (1939–1945). Steam engines cost a lot to operate. Pollution from the coal was harmful to the environment. They were no longer able to compete with the new electric- and diesel-powered locomotives. Gasoline and oil were used in locomotives for a while. Oil-powered locomotives could not pull heavy loads. Gas engines were expensive to operate.

Train engineers of the past would be shocked to see the Shinkansen, one of Japan's famed Maglev trains.

Businesses wanted locomotives to go faster and use less fuel. Engineers were challenged to find better designs.

Rudolph Diesel invented a new engine in 1892. He powered the engine with diesel fuel. Diesel fuel is different than gasoline. It is distilled and will not ignite if you light it. By the mid-1920s, engineers joined diesel fuel and electric power in locomotive engines. Heavy freight loads could be pulled using a diesel-electric engine with less pollution and cost.

Electricity changed train travel. Electric locomotives were lighter and traveled quickly over long distances at higher speeds. Trains using electricity could travel on tracks above or below ground. Single cars carried passengers around town using cables. Train travel became more versatile.

Japan was the first country to install high-speed rail systems, or HSRs, in 1964. This train was named the bullet train. These trains run on standard rails. Trains can speed across the countryside at 120 to 160 mph. Because they go so fast, engineers must make changes to the track system design. Routes need wider curves and better braking systems. Automobiles sitting at crossings need to be warned sooner.

The most exciting new discovery occurred in 1984 when engineers opened the first magnetic levitation, or Maglev, people mover. Using a combination of electricity and magnets, trains "float" above a track. These early people movers inspired engineers to create Maglev trains that are very fast.

As trains become more technical and as the world changes, new and increasingly difficult problems will have to be solved. Engineers will continue to ask questions and devise solutions for exciting new ways of transporting people and goods by rail.

2

All Aboard!

Imagine if there was a heavy box sitting on the floor and it needed to be moved from one room to another. How could it be moved? How much energy would it take to move it? How much work would have to be done to get it moved to where it needed to go?

Energy is an action and a force. It can't be seen or touched. It is not an object like a truck or car. The same amount of energy is always available. It can be stored in objects or it may change forms. Engineers figure out ways to change energy into a form that can help people work with less effort. Engines are machines that have helped people work.

How do engines take energy and move things? Engines use fuel, pressure, heat, and combustion to change energy into motion. Combustion, or burning, is a chemical reaction that makes heat.

Think about what is needed to start a campfire. First, you need a fuel that will burn. Heat must be applied to the fuel, usually in the form of fire. Air must be present, too. When all three things are together, the fuel ignites, or catches on fire and burns. As more fuel, heat, and air are added to the fire, it gets bigger. If this fire was squeezed into a small container, the pressure put on the fire would make it hotter.

This process occurs in engines. Energy can move wheels, gears, and pistons. If an engine is put in a locomotive it will carry freight or people quickly to faraway places.

Steam Engines

In 1825, when George Stephenson engineered his first steam locomotive, little did he know that he was going to transform the world. This invention took a plentiful source of fuel, such as coal or wood, and turned it into mechanical energy.

Mechanical energy is the ability of something to work or to move. This meant that the steam locomotive could do the work of many men. More coal could be mined and hauled to the sea. Factories far away from the mines could have more coal to fuel their machines. Steam locomotives could move much more weight much quicker than a horse-drawn cart.

Steam locomotives were complicated machines. They burned wood or coal in a fireproof box. This firebox had pipes that extended into a large container called a boiler. The boiler was filled with water. Pipes extended from the firebox into the boiler. When the pipes became hot, the water got hot. When the water was hot enough, it turned into steam.

Think about what happens when water is put into a squirt gun. The water goes into a large cylinder and sloshes around with no direction or force. It doesn't have any power until that water goes into a small tube and is squeezed out under pressure through a small opening. The same thing happens with the steam in a locomotive.

The water in the boiler is super heated to a temperature of over 212° F (100° C). When water turns to steam it expands. As the steam expands, it moves into a smaller steam pipe. This pipe leads into a cylinder. In the cylinder is a plunger called a piston. The piston is connected to a straight rod. The straight rod is connected to a wheel.

A cross-section of a steam engine from the late 1800s shows how fire heats tubes of water to create the steam needed to power the engine.

As the steam floods into the cylinder under pressure, it pushes the piston back and forth. This moves the rod and turns the wheel.

The steam engine was a workhorse, but it had problems. The engine was very heavy because it was made of iron. In the early years, its weight broke the iron rails of the tracks. Engineers solved this by adding more wheels to the locomotive. This distributed the weight over the whole length of the locomotive.

Sometimes the firebox in the locomotive became very hot. It could get so hot that the firebox exploded. If the engineer got hurt and was not able to control the train, the train might derail. Inventors solved this problem by inserting a lead plug at the top of the firebox. If the box got too hot the plug would melt and warn the attendant.

Steam locomotives sent a lot of smoke into the air. Newer engines did not pollute as much. The fuels that powered steam engines became scarce and expensive. In the 1950s, diesel-powered locomotives replaced steam locomotives. After many years of service, steam locomotives were retired from active service.

The Atmospheric Railroad

In 1847, an "atmospheric" railroad opened in England. The train, invented by Isambard Brunel, used a steam engine placed next to a single rail. The steam engine powered a central piston that was under the train. The piston pulled the train cars without using a locomotive. The cars were pulled for 3 miles (4.8 km) then had to be handed off to another steam engine–powered piston. The train ran at an incredible speed of 68 mph (1110 kph). That was very fast for this time period. The idea did not last long. Horses had to tow the train to get started. Also, people thought that rats liked to chew on the leather parts of the cylinder.

Diesel Engines

Steam and diesel engines work in very similar ways. Steam engines are external combustion engines. That means that the combustion or burning of the fuel happens outside of the engine and heats a tube. The tube then gives the heat to the water inside of the boiler. This is called a heat exchange.

Diesel engines are internal combustion engines. They take the fuel and heat it inside the engine. All the energy stays inside the engine. This makes internal combustion engines more powerful and

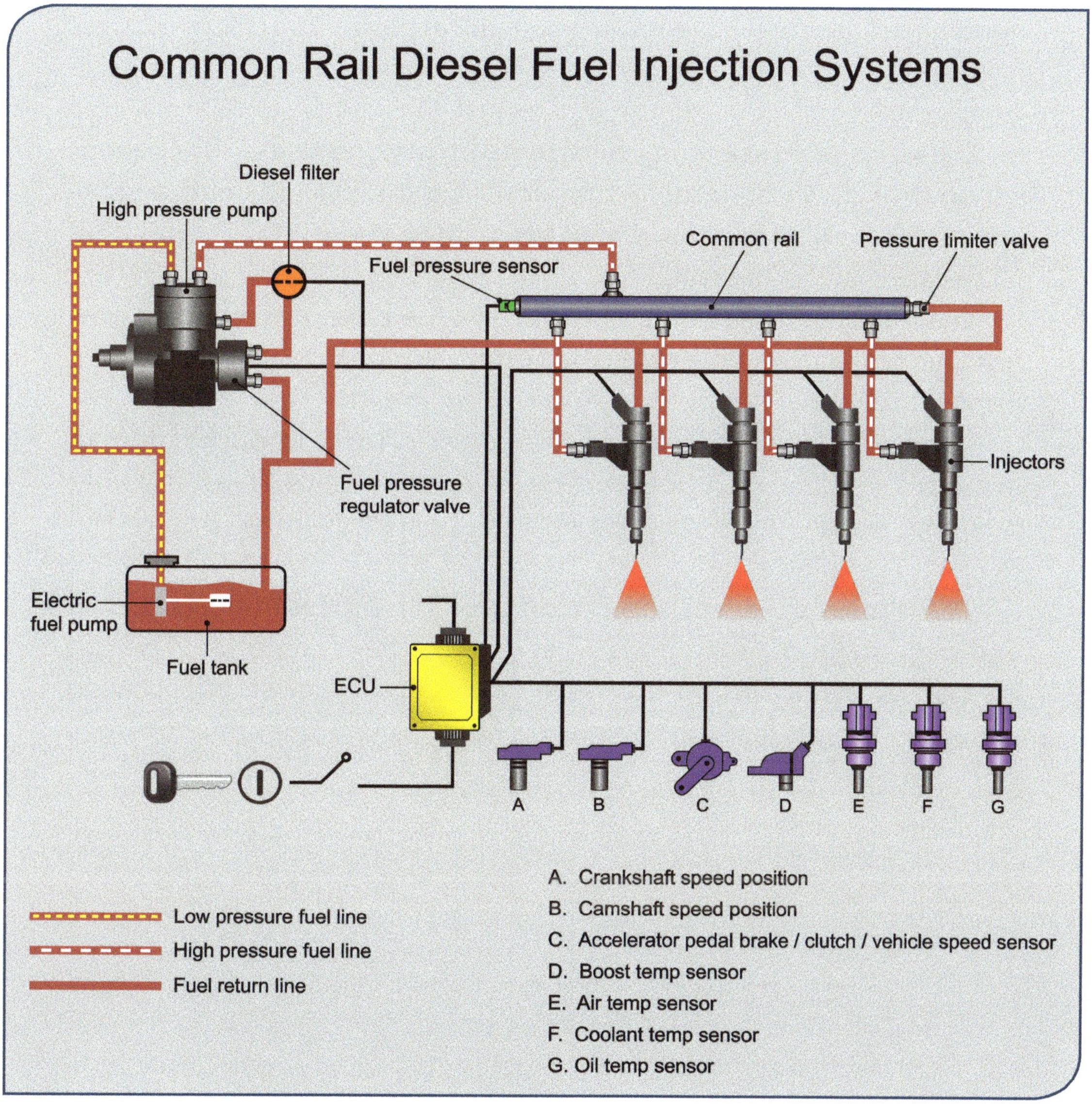

Diesel engines are powered by pressurized fuel, which is injected and then ignited inside pistons.

efficient. They have fewer parts so they don't break easily. They are lighter because they have fewer mechanical parts. Diesel locomotives use less fuel and haul heavier loads. This makes them less expensive to operate.

Diesel engines use many cylinders with pistons inside. The pistons go up and down squeezing the air inside the cylinder into a small space. When this happens, the air heats up to about 1,000° F (537.77° C) because of the pressure!

Imagine blowing air into a balloon. As the balloon expands it gets hot. Air molecules are pushed together. When the balloon is full it pops. This is what happens inside a diesel engine.

Air travels into a cylinder in the engine. A piston pushes the air into a small space. As it gets compressed, it heats up. At just the right moment, diesel fuel is sprayed into the heated cylinder. Boom! The diesel fuel explodes.

The explosion drives the piston up. This process happens over and over again. This action is what powers the locomotive. The gas created by the explosion is expelled out of the cylinder and is called exhaust. This gas leaves the engine and goes into the atmosphere.

3

Magnets and More

In the twentieth century, cars and trucks began to replace trains. Cars had become affordable and available. Trucks carried freight directly to their destinations, unlike trains or ships. Gas was plentiful. America's highway system was expanded and improved. When the oil crisis occurred in the 1970s, oil became scarce. Trains that used electricity for power were the solution.

Trolleys, Cable Cars, and Subways

Engineers realized very early that magnets could generate electricity. In 1837, a chemist in Scotland built an electric locomotive. Large batteries powered the motor inside the locomotive. He discovered that this kind of electrical motor was not very powerful. Soon, the locomotive was destroyed and forgotten.

Scientists continued to look for ways to make trains go faster. In 1879, the electric lightbulb was invented. It demonstrated how clean and inexpensive electricity could be. Soon, engineers realized that trains could be powered by electricity. That was achieved through an overhead line or an electrified third rail, which rain along the train's route.

Eventually, many new kinds of trains were developed. Cable cars ran on streets in San Francisco. These cars hung from a single rail and were powered by electricity. Subways took trains underground. Electric-powered streetcars ran on rails and connected neighborhoods in large cities. Interurban railways took passengers from one town to another.

Every steam and diesel locomotive that traveled sent soot, sparks, and carbon gases into the air wherever they went. However, electricity

Electricity helped cable cars in San Francisco, California, and other cities to transport citizens more efficiently and with less cost, noise, and pollution than steam locomotives.

for a city was made at a power station. It ran through electric lines wherever it needed to go. Engineers found that electricity could move freight and people quickly, quietly, cheaply, and without a lot of pollution.

High-Speed Rails

The rail industry has always been obsessed with speed. There is no real definition for a high-speed rail (HSR) system. It seems that any train that can travel at speeds between 90 to 220 mph (145 to 354 kph) is considered a HSR. New designs in diesel-electric engines help some locomotives go faster. Many HSRs use overhead electric lines to power the locomotives. Physical laws limit how fast trains can go. Problems like the angle of curves, time needed to stop a train, and passenger comfort and safety must be overcome before they can go faster.

Engineers have experimented with designing a locomotive so that air moves around it with little wind resistance. Japan Railways designed their locomotives with small, round "noses." They are called bullet trains because the trains look like bullets. This design helps lessen wind resistance, which makes them able to travel from 161 to 186 mph (259 to 299 kph)! That speed is more than two times faster than automobiles drive on highways.

Most high-speed rail trains have from eight to sixteen cars. These cars are permanently hooked together. This group of cars is called a train set. At the front of the train set is the locomotive. It is usually powered by an overhead electric line. Some companies add traction motors to almost every car, which help the train start and stop more efficiently. A new traction motor design using a permanent magnet motor uses less energy than older traction motors. More wheels on the track make for a smoother ride for passengers.

HSR trains go faster if they travel on a flat, straight track. Rail routes with fewer curves allow trains to stay at higher speeds for the longest amount of time. When a train goes around a curve it experiences centrifugal force. Imagine riding a roller coaster as it goes around a curve at a high speed. That force you feel is centrifugal force. If the roller coaster goes around the curve too quickly or the curve is too tight it will fly off the track. HSR trains will do that, too.

Magnetic Levitation

Magnetic levitation, or maglev, trains use magnets to move them. They use a special motor called a linear induction motor. This invention appeared in the early 1900s. An English professor from Imperial College, Eric Laithwaite, was the first electrical engineer to develop a working linear induction engine.

His motor used electromagnetic induction to make things move. Electromagnetic induction happens when you move magnets around a coil of wire that then makes electricity. The wires carry the electricity to power the motor.

German engineers have designed the ICE (InterCity Express) trains to transport people between cities at speeds up to 186 mph (300 kmh).

The aerodynamic design of this Japanese Maglev train allows it to slip through the air with little resistance. This 30-ton train can travel over 361 mph (581 kmh).

Here's how it works. All magnets have a north pole and a south pole. Like poles repel, while opposite poles attract. With electromagnetic induction, the electricity is made in the metal coils when the two poles of the magnets rotate from repelling each other to attracting each other.

To make trains move, super-magnetized coils are attached on the inside of the outer rails. Large magnets are attached to the underside of the train. As the magnets repel and attract each other the train floats above the track and moves. Maglev trains have no wheels touching the track. Because there is no friction holding the train back, they can travel incredibly fast. Maglev trains slow down and stop by moving the magnets closer to or farther away from the track.

The whole train is designed to slip through the air with little resistance. Maglev trains have reached speeds of more than 310 mph (499 kph). An airplane can fly at a speed of about 562 mph (904.5 kph). Imagine flying along the ground on a train that goes nearly as fast as an airplane. The human body's limitations determine how fast a maglev can start and stop.

Shipyard Monorail

English engineers wondered how to move goods around a worksite. Henry Robinson Palmer solved the problem in 1824. He built a one-railed system in a shipyard. His monorail put carriages full of freight in the center of a single track above the ground. Horses pulled it along the rail. It kept the freight above the ground and out of the way. The next year at a factory in London, he built the Chestnut Railway to pull passengers. It carried passengers three months before George Stephenson's steam locomotive carried passengers on the Stockton and Darlington line.

Maglev technology moves trains quickly but can go slowly enough to move commuters around a city. This helps with traffic, noise, and pollution in large urban areas. Some cities use a maglev monorail system at airports. Tel Aviv, Israel, is installing an elevated, hanging train called SkyTran. The spaceship-like pods hold two people and will eventually travel at 60 mph (96.56 kph) to any place in the city.

4

Riding the Rails

From the earliest recorded instance of a human using a wheeled cart on a track, engineers have struggled with problems concerning how to move more people and freight. What safety and comfort issues are important? What track material will not break under heavy weights? What is the best way to join cars together so that they don't derail on curves? What kind of braking system will stop a heavy train safely? Engineers have used the answers to these questions to make many improvements to trains and tracks.

Passenger Cars

On early train trips, passengers stood on an open-air, wooden platform covered only by a roof. Small holes in the floor drained the rainwater. Eventually, enclosed wooden benches that held six people were installed.

Some early steam trains simply attached a group of stagecoaches together. Flanged wheels that fit on the metal tracks replaced the regular wheels. That is why passenger cars are called coaches or carriages. Currently, some countries call a train car frame a bogie. The wheels and support for the train car are attached to this frame.

Instead of diesel fuel, this solar train uses solar panels to power the lights, fans, and information panels. Solar energy saves money and the environment.

Trains with steam engines and wooden cars were not only uncomfortable but were not very safe. They would break apart or catch on fire easily if the train derailed.

Now when a passenger steps on a train, the car is made of steel, is enclosed, and has padded seats. Train cars are strong and safe. They are equipped with air-conditioning and bathrooms. Special cars are available where travelers can eat, sleep, or view the countryside. Now, the bogies have shock absorbers attached to them and better couplings to help absorb the movement of the cars.

Freight Cars

Freight cars are just passenger cars without the frills. Their designs have been changed as the kind of freight or goods they carry has changed. Businesses that use trains to move their freight are concerned about cost. Engineers work to design freight cars that are strong and light at the same time. If the train weighs less it costs the customer less to ship freight. Also, heavy loads move slower and use more fuel.

Locomotives must be powerful enough to pull heavy loads up hills. They have to stop quickly and safely. Since they transport freight long distances, their brakes, car bodies, and couplers must be stronger than in passenger cars.

Early freight cars were made of wood, then changed to iron, then to steel. Steel is strong, light, and durable. Originally, cars were designed with sides but without roofs and were used to haul heavy ore. Eventually, enclosed boxcars were designed for items that required protection from the weather. Covered gondolas (cars with v-shaped sides) carried grain, coal, and other materials. Engineers looked at the characteristics of what needed to be hauled and designed special cars. Today, freight cars come in all shapes and sizes. They move everything from mail to medicine.

A Solar Train?

In New Delhi, India, some passenger cars look different than most. That is because engineers installed solar panels on top of six cars. The panels collect sunlight and change it into electricity, which is stored in batteries. Although a diesel locomotive still pulls the train, the solar panels will produce electricity for the lights, displays, and fans in the passenger cars. The railway hopes to save $20,000 per year and reduce pollution by using less diesel fuel.

Freight cars are designed with strong steel sides to move cargo without damage.

Rails and Tracks

Early wooden rails wore out quickly. Iron straps placed on top of the rails increased durability. Engineers discovered that heavy freight cars broke the brittle iron straps. When steel was discovered, engineers found that rails could be rolled out in large sheets. Also, steel was smooth and easy to shape. Train wheels rolled over with less resistance, and trains traveled faster.

Many rail designs were developed for different situations. As more and more tracks were laid, engineers encountered unique problems with curves. If tracks were laid with one rail higher than the other on curves, it counteracted centrifugal force. Braking at the right speed while going around curves kept the train from derailing.

Gauge, or the width from the inside edge of one rail to the other, varied due to the differing widths of carts and bogies. Engineers worked to find which gauge was best. Smaller gauge tracks were less expensive to build but trains had to travel slower and be lighter. Wider gauges allowed trains to use higher speeds and carry heavier loads but cost more. Currently, most railways are now standardized at a gauge of 4 feet, 8.5 inches (1.42 meters).

Stopping, Starting, and Staying Together

Early train cars were coupled together by chains and had no brakes on the individual cars. When the horses or locomotive stopped the train, all the cars would bump together. Since early trains did not travel very quickly, no one got hurt but it was uncomfortable.

Engineers discovered that having brakes on every car was very important. If a car became uncoupled from the train for any reason, without a brake it could not be stopped or even held in place.

As trains hauled heavier loads and moved at faster speeds, stopping safely and quickly was very important. As a train stops, it needs to release energy. Engineers needed to know how much pressure to apply to the wheels and when to start applying that pressure so that it would stop safely. If a bicycle is ridden downhill, the person riding must discover how and when to apply the brakes at the right time to stop at the bottom. They test the amount of pressure to apply to the brakes so that they will not crash. If brakes are applied too quickly and with too much pressure, the bicycle will skid and crash. Engineers had to discover this same thing.

As steam trains developed, brakes were placed on all the cars. Each car had its own brakeman who turned a wheel, which applied pressure to the brakes on the car. If the brakeman didn't turn the wheel in time the train would not stop. Soon, engineers designed brakes for each car that used the steam from the locomotive to stop the train.

By the mid-1800s brakes were not the only thing that had improved. Trains had couplers that connected cars with a stiff pin and loop. They kept the cars from bumping together. These couplers were dangerous, and many injuries occurred as trains backed up and slammed together as workers pinned the cars together. During the Civil War, Eli Janney realized that there was a safer way to couple cars together. His coupler looks like two hands clasping together with an automatic pin in the middle. It is called a knuckle coupler, and he received a patent for it in 1873.

Air brakes on trains are designed to stop each car smoothly, which keeps passengers and freight safe and undamaged.

Modern trains still use the basic design of the knuckle coupler but have improved it to keep cars from coming apart in derailments. Brakes, however, have greatly improved with the introduction of electricity. George Westinghouse designed an air brake that sent compressed air evenly to the brakes so that all the wheels stopped together. There were fewer accidents and, by 1880, his brake design was the standard on most trains. It is still in use today.

5

Hyperloop to Flying Trains: What's Next?

Trains must advance as the world gets smaller and people travel more. Trains are an efficient and effective way for freight and people to travel. In the future, people will live in cities farther away from their jobs. Highways will have many more cars on them. Cities may be polluted and the air hard to breathe. Machines will need to work better and use cleaner fuel. Scientists are concerned about fossil fuel emissions from gas and diesel engines. Many countries are trying to cut these emissions because of global climate change. Engineers who design the trains of the future will need to solve these problems. Already, some very exciting new trains are being developed.

Electrically Powered Fuel Cell Locomotives

Future trains may use locomotives powered by a fuel cell. A fuel cell is like a battery. This new technology will use a chemical reaction inside the fuel cell to power the locomotive. A chemical reaction takes place when molecules combine together to create something different. Something happens when they combine. If a piece of rock candy is dropped into a glass of water, the chemical reaction creates bubbles and releases energy.

Water and steam are the only emissions from this German-designed hydrogen-powered train, which uses fuel cells to convert hydrogen into electricity.

A hydrail uses a combination of hydrogen and oxygen to power the locomotive. A chemical reaction happens inside the fuel cell when the hydrogen and oxygen are mixed together. This reaction creates energy and sends it to the batteries. The batteries then power the engine. Engineers hope that this type of fuel will replace diesel fuel in trains of the future.

Locomotives that use hydrogen fuel produce only steam and water. Also, this engine is very quiet. Any extra electricity is stored in the batteries and used later. This new engine design will fit in current

A representative of the National Organisation Hydrogen and Fuel Cell Technology proudly displays a representation of a hydrogen train.

diesel engines. German engineers plan to have this new, green engine in use by 2018.

Vactrains

In the early 1860s, Alfred Ely Beach had a vision. He sat in his office in New York City and saw lots of traffic. He wondered if he could invent an underground transportation system. Could he build a tunnel under the streets and put a carriage in it? How much air would it take to push

The First Vacuum Train

In 1799, George Medhurst of London thought up a great idea. He wondered if air forced through a tube would move objects. If the air in the tube was squeezed tighter, would the object travel faster? He discovered that objects would go faster. He was the first engineer to imagine a transportation system that used air in a tube. His vacuum train idea was never built. Engineers continue to experiment with this idea.

a carriage full of people? He was an inventor and soon learned about vacuum tubes. In 1867, he displayed his invention at the American Institute Fair. His above-ground tube was 6 feet (1.8 m) around and 10 feet (3 m) long. A large fan attached to the end of it pushed a small car inside the tube. People loved his new idea!

Current ideas for vacuum train systems came from this very idea. Robert Goddard, who developed the modern rocket, had an idea for a vactrain in 1909. Later, engineers designed vactrains that used pressurized air, fans, and a vacuum to move cars through a tube. Imagine if a small object was placed in a straw. When air is blown strongly through the straw that object will fly out of the straw very fast! The object can move on the cushioned bed of air with very little friction. With nothing to resist its forward movement it will move quickly. This basic idea is behind most vactrain designs.

Since building the tube system is very costly, modern engineers think that a trainset rail system that uses magnetic levitation will solve more transportation problems than vactrains. Today, there are no vactrain transportation systems operating anywhere in the world. Also, no one knows if the idea will work for long-distance travel. However, engineers around the world are working together to make vactrain travel a reality. Engineer, businessman, and inventor

Elon Musk has challenged the world to help him design these train systems. Engineers hope that these systems using renewable fuel will help reduce pollution.

The Hyperloop and More

It has been four years since Elon Musk challenged engineers to design a train travel system that would suck pods through a tube. He called his idea the Hyperloop. Pneumatic tubes would hurl pods through a tube or magnets would pull them at very high speeds. They would travel so fast that a trip from Los Angeles to San Francisco would take thirty minutes.

The passenger pods would travel through a large tube. Some engineers think these trains could go 700 mph (1,126 kph). Passengers will board a pod that looks like a spaceship. Seats will be padded with headrests. The amount of energy and time required to launch and stop a pod traveling at 700 mph are problems that engineers are working to solve. Pods would travel smoothly on a cushion of air like an airplane. They could also be pulled by magnets. They might even use some new technology that no one has thought of yet!

A company called Hyperloop One built a model of the system in Nevada that uses maglev technology. In July of 2017, a pod successfully traveled through a tube at 70 mph (112 kph). The company hopes it will soon travel at 250 mph (402 kph).

Chinese scientists are designing a maglev train system that would run in a vacuum tube underwater. The tube would be held up by a floating bridge or travel in underwater tunnels. The tube would reduce air resistance, allowing the train to move faster. This is just an idea right now but China has constructed many underwater tunnels in the past. So, in the future, passengers might experience a 6-mile, 1,243-mph (9.6-km, 2,000-kmh) trip in a tube underwater. This super-maglev train could be three times faster than an airplane.

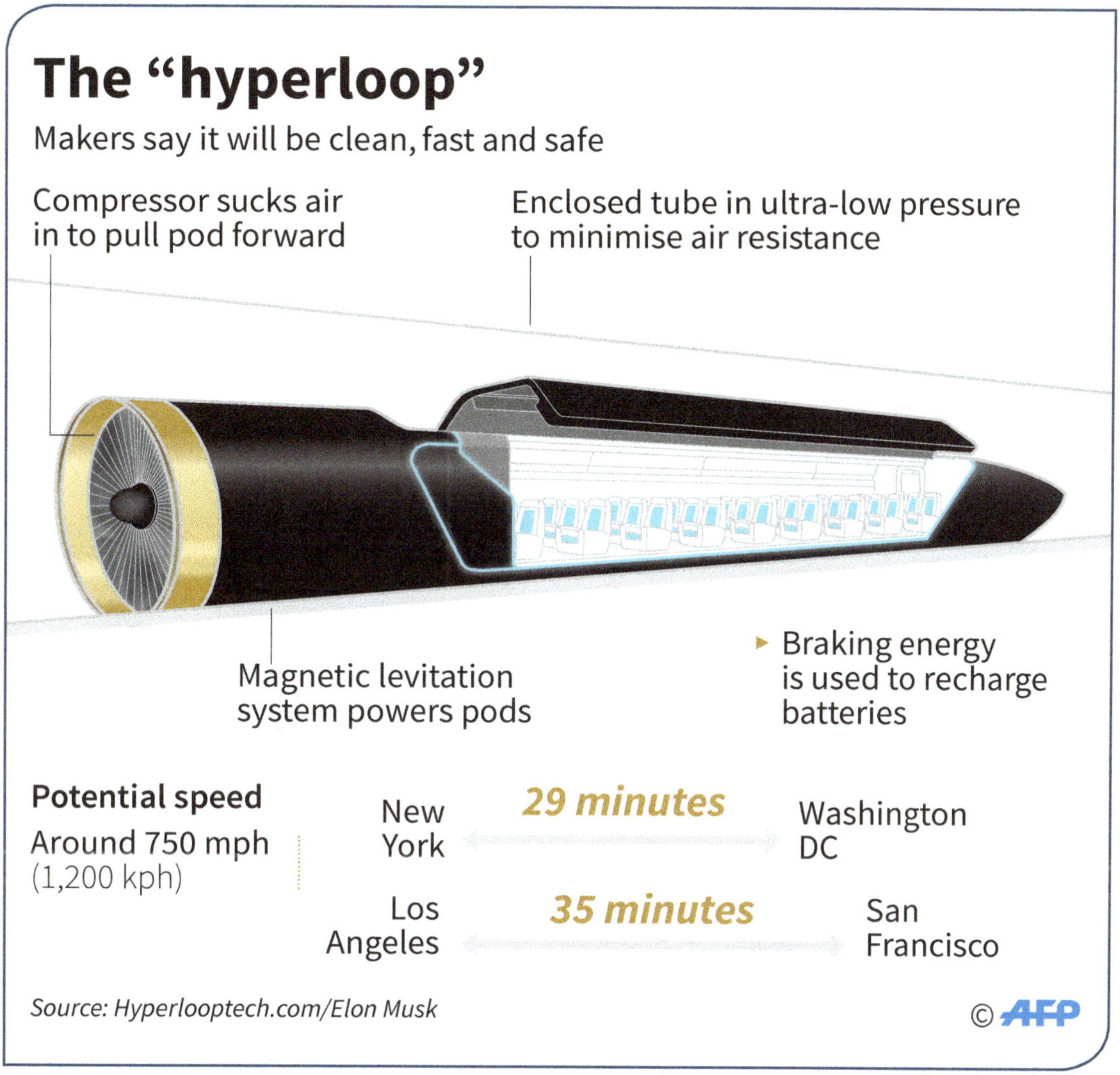

A look at an engineering design for the Hyperloop train

Into the Future

There are so many exciting possibilities for rail transport in the future. Only the mind will limit where scientists take humanity. Many engineers will work together to solve modern problems. People will want to travel around the world. How will they do that using renewable energy and with little pollution? Everyday trips to the store, which may be 50 miles away (80 km), may take only minutes. Right now a Swiss company is designing a flying train. It flies like an airplane but will pick up and move three pods of freight or people. Instead of transporting only freight or only people, a flying train will do both. It is innovative thinking like this that will help move the world forward while protecting water, air, and land.

CHRONOLOGY

600 BCE–800 CE

Greeks develop a system of dug-out tracks that fit wagons and carts.

1784

James Watt patents a design for a steam engine using high-pressure steam technology.

1803

Richard Trevithick builds the first steam railway locomotive.

1824

George Stephenson builds the Locomotion No. 1, capable of pulling 90 tons (81 metric tons) of coal at 15 mph (24 kph).

1827

Baltimore and Ohio Railroad starts building the first railroad in America.

1865

The Pullman sleeping car is introduced in the United States.

1869

The first transcontinental railway is completed.

1872

American inventor George Westinghouse patents his first automatic air brake.

1917

GE produces an experimental diesel-electric locomotive.

1940s

Eric Laithwaite builds the first full-size linear induction engine.

1964

Bullet train service is introduced in Japan.

2007

High-speed trains that travel at 217 mph (349 kph) are introduced in Spain.

2013

Elon Musk introduces idea of the Hyperloop.

2014

Design work for the Tel Aviv SkyTran begins.

2017

Hyperloop One completes its first full-scale test of hyperloop technology.

BIBLIOGRAPHY

"A History of Railroad Couplers." American-Rails.com. Retrieved October 1, 2017. http://www.american-rails.com/couplers.html.

"Brakes." The Railway Technical Website. Retrieved September 15, 2017. http://www.railway-technical.com/trains/rolling-stock-index-l/train-equipment/brakes.

"Electromagnetic Induction Lesson for Kids." Study.com. Retrieved September 16, 2016. http://www.study.com/academy/lesson/electromagnetic-induction-lesson-for-kids.html.

GCR Staff. "Shares Plunge Again as Carillion Issues New Profit Warning; Covenants to Be Breached." Global Construction Review, June 17, 2017. http://www.globalconstructionreview.com/news/chinese-scie7ntists-prop7ose-2000kmh-sub7marine.

Hawkins, Andrew J. "The World's First Hydrogen-Powered Passenger Train Is Coming to Germany." The Verge, September 23, 2016. http://www.theverge.com/2016/9/23/13022400/hydrogen-train-germany-coradia-ilint-alstom-innotrans.

Herring, Peter. *Ultimate Train*. Don Mills, ON: Oxford University Press, 2000.

Molloy, Mark. "The Future of Travel? First Photos of Hyperloop Test Track Built in Nevada Desert." *Telegraph*, March 21, 2017. http://www.telegraph.co.uk/technology/2017/03/07/future-travel-first-photos-hyperloop-test-track-built-nevada.

Swapna, Krishna. "India's First Solar-Powered Train Makes Its Debut." Engaget, July 18, 2017. http://www.engadget.com/2017/07/18/india-first-solar-powered-train.

"Video - Clip-Air, the 'flying train.'" Aeronewstv.com, October 7, 2015. http://www.aeronewstv.com/en/industry/research-innovation/2698-clip-air-the-flying-train.html.

Westwood, J. N. *The Historical Atlas of World Railroads*. Richmond Hill, ON: Firefly Books, 2009.

Withuhn, William L. "Locomotive." World Book, 2017. http://www.worldbookonline.com/academic/article?id=ar328540.

Woodford, Chris. "Diesel Engines." Explain That Stuff!, October 22, 2017. http://www.explainthatstuff.com/diesel-engines.html.

GLOSSARY

bogie A metal platform underneath a train where wheelsets are attached.

centrifugal force A force on an object moving in a circular path that makes the object move out and away from its center.

combustion A chemical reaction where something combines with oxygen to produce heat and light.

coupling A joint that hooks train cars together.

emissions Anything, like a gas or steam, that is released out into the open.

flanged wheel Rimmed edge that keeps a wheel on a rail.

friction The action of one surface rubbing against another.

gauge The width from the inside edge of one rail to the other.

generator An engine that changes mechanical energy into electrical energy by electromagnetic induction.

gondola A train car that is open on the top.

hybrid A mixture of two different things, resulting in something that has a little bit of both

levitation Suspending an object in the air.

magnetic levitation (maglev) A train that is suspended on a magnetic cushion above a magnetized track and travels free of friction.

piston A short cylinder fitted into a larger cylinder that moves up and down against a liquid or gas.

steel A strong metal used for trains that combines iron with other elements.

FURTHER READING

Books

Harris, Michael, and Steve Parker. *Exploring Science: Trains with 10 Easy-to-Do Experiments and 230 Exciting Pictures*. London, UK: Armadillo, 2016.

Otfinoski, Steven. *High-Speed Trains: From Concept to Consumer*. New York, NY: Children's Press, 2016.

Spilsbury, Louise. *Maglev Trains*. New York, NY: Gareth Stevens Publishing, 2016.

West, David. *Trains* (Mechanic Mike's Machines). London, UK: Franklin Watts, 2016.

Websites

DKfindout!

www.dkfindout.com/uk/transport/history-trains

Interactive website with clickable links and information about the history of trains.

Easy Science for Kids

www.easyscienceforkids.com/all-about-trains

A science website for kids with information about train history and other science subjects.

Kids Discover

www.online.kidsdiscover.com

This website allows searches on various topics from early to modern trains; a large amount of encyclopedic information in a kid-friendly format.

INDEX